For Melanie Pirotta – S.G.

For Nick, Cathryn and Steven, with love – S.A.

Text copyright © 2002 Sam Godwin
Illustrations copyright © 2002 Simone Abel
Volume copyright © 2002 Hodder Wayland

Series concept and design: Liz Black
Book design: Jane Hawkins
Commissioning Editor: Lisa Edwards
Editor: Katie Orchard
Science Consultant: Dr Carol Ballard

Published in Great Britain in 2002 as All Kinds of Everything by Hodder Wayland,
an imprint of Hodder Children's Books

This paperback edition published in 2009 by Wayland,
an imprint of Hachette Children's Books,
338 Euston Road, London NW1 3BH
www.hachettelivre.co.uk

The right of Sam Godwin to be identified as the author
and the right of Simone Abel to be identified as the
illustrator of this Work has been asserted by them in
accordance with the Copyright, Designs and Patents Act 1988.

Cataloguing in publication data
Godwin, Sam
It's a Material World: a first look at materials. – (Little Bees)
1. Materials – Pictorial works – Juvenile literature
    I. Title
    620.1'1

ISBN 978 07502 5879 1

Printed and bound in China

It's a Material World

A first look at materials

It's a Material World
A first look at materials

Sam Godwin

WAYLAND

Everything around us is

Ow! I didn't see that coming!

It's made of glass, Titch. You can see through it, but it's a solid material.

made of different materials.

Hey, this window's open! Let's go in.

Materials can be solid or liquid.

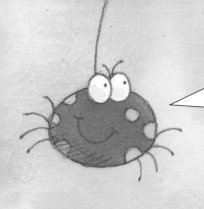

My web is soft and bendy, just like jelly!

Hey, Zip, can you stretch everything like jelly?

No, Titch. Some hard materials, like glass, can't stretch.

There are hard solids and soft ones.

Liquids flow freely, like water.

You can pour liquids into some solid objects.

My tummy can hold a lot of liquid. If only I can get to it!

Zip, could this paper bag hold water?

No, some materials, like paper, aren't waterproof.

15

Materials change when they become hot.

Oh, no! I'm getting wet!

Water becomes steam.

Steam changes back into water when it cools down.

I hope that chocolate doesn't change into anything else before I get there!

Some solids, like jelly cubes, dissolve in water.

Stirring helps the jelly to dissolve.

Why is the lady using the wooden spoon instead of the shiny one?

20

Wow! The ice is floating.

Liquids turn into solids when they become cold.

Water freezes and turns into ice.

The warm orange juice will melt the ice.

Some materials change when they cool down.

Hey, this chocolate has turned solid again!

It takes all kinds of materials to make up a world.

Wow! It looks like all those materials have turned into a party!

All about materials

We use lots of different materials every day, such as wood, paper, metal, plastic, glass, sand, stone, wool or cloth.

Some materials are natural and some are made by people.

Solids can be hard or soft.

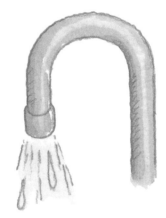

Materials can be solid or liquid.

You can pour some liquids into some solid objects.

Some materials melt when they become hot.

Liquids freeze when they become cold.

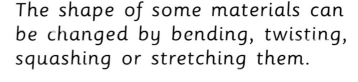

The shape of some materials can be changed by bending, twisting, squashing or stretching them.

Useful Words

Dissolve
When a solid, such as sugar, disapppears into a liquid, such as water.

Freeze
When a liquid becomes so cold it turns into a solid. Water becomes ice when it freezes.

Melt
When a solid, such as jelly, is heated and turns into a liquid.

Transparent
See-through.

You will see lots of different types of materials at home or at school. Find out which of them are:

warm   squashy   shiny   cold

stretchy   transparent   magnetic

hard   bendy   wobbly   rough

twisty   smooth   bendy   soft

able to float   hot   dull